Anonymous

Eine unparteiische Liedersammlung

Zum Gebrauch beim öffentlichen Gottesdienst und der häuslichen Erbauung

Anonymous

Eine unparteiische Liedersammlung
Zum Gebrauch beim öffentlichen Gottesdienst und der häuslichen Erbauung

ISBN/EAN: 9783743415638

Hergestellt in Europa, USA, Kanada, Australien, Japan

Cover: Foto ©Thomas Meinert / pixelio.de

Manufactured and distributed by brebook publishing software (www.brebook.com)

Anonymous

Eine unparteiische Liedersammlung

THE UNION HARP:

ORIGINAL AND SELECTED;

BY

EDWIN BURNHAM.

PHILADELPHIA:
1861.

THE UNION HARP.

1.

1 Praise God from whom all blessings flow;
Praise him all creatures here below;
Praise him above, ye heavenly host;
Praise Father, Son, and Holy Ghost.

2 Praise him whose mighty throne is high;
Whose robes are light and majesty;
Whose terrors keep the world in awe;
Whose justice guards his holy law.

3 Great is the Lord, and great his might!
Kind are his ways, his judgments right;
In love he builds his holy throne,
And ever makes his mercy known.

4 Through all his works his wisdom shines,
And baffles Satan's deep designs;
His power is sovereign to fulfil
The noblest counsels of his will.

2.

1 All hail the great Immanuel's name!
Let angels prostrate fall!
Bring forth the royal diadem,
And crown him Lord of all!

Let Gentile sinners not forget.
Who saves them from the fall;
Go spread your trophies at his feet,
And crown him Lord of all!

3 Ye chosen seed of Israel's race—
  A remnant weak and small—
Hail him who saves you by his grace,
  And crown him Lord of all!

4 Let every kindred, every tribe,
  On this terrestrial ball,
To him all majesty ascribe,
  And crown him Lord of all!

5 O, that with yonder sacred throng
  I at his feet may fall,
And join the everlasting song,
  And crown him Lord of all!

3. S. M.

1 Awake, and sing the song
  Of Moses and the Lamb;
Wake, every heart and every tongue,
  To praise the Saviour's name.

2 Sing of his dying love;
  Sing of his rising power;
Sing how he intercedes above
  For those whose sins he bore.

3 Sing on your heavenly way,
  Ye ransomed sinners, sing;
Sing on, rejoicing every day
  In Christ, your glorious King.

4 Soon shall we hear him say,
  "Ye blessed children, come!"
Soon will he call us all away
  To our eternal home.

5 Then shall our raptured tongue
  His endless praise proclaim,
And sweeter voices tune the song
  Of Moses and the Lamb.

4.

1 O Thou from whom all goodness flows,
  I lift my soul to thee;
 In all my conflicts, fears, and woes,
  Do thou remember me.

2 When trials sore obstruct my way,
  And ills I cannot flee;
 O, let my strength be as my day;
  Do thou remember me.

3 If, for thy sake, upon my name
  Reproach and shame shall be,
 I welcome both reproach and shame;
  Do thou remember me.

4 And when before thy throne I stand,
  And all thy glory see,
 O, bid me pass to thy right hand;
  O, then remember me!

5.

1 Jesus, refuge of my soul,
  Let me to thy bosom fly,
 While the raging billows roll,
  While the tempest still is high;
 Hide me, O my Saviour, hide,
  Till the storm of life is past!
 Safe into the haven guide,
  And receive me at the last.

2 Other refuge have I none;
  Hangs my helpless soul on thee;
 Leave, O, leave me not alone!
  Still support and comfort me;
 All my trust on thee is stayed,
  All my help from thee I bring;
 Cover my defenceless head
  With the shadow of thy wing.

3 Thou, O Christ, art all I want;
   All in all in thee I find;
Raise the fallen, cheer the faint,
   Heal the sick, and lead the blind.
Just and holy is thy name;
   Thine is perfect righteousness.
Save me from my sin and shame;
   Fill me with thy truth and grace.

6.   L. M.

1 O Thou, to whose all-searching sight
The darkness shineth as the light,
Search, prove my heart, it pants for thee:
O, burst these bonds and set it free.

2 Wash out its stains, refine its dross;
Nail my affections to the cross;
Hallow each thought, let all within
Be clean, as thou, my Lord, art clean.

3 If in this darksome wild I stray,
Be thou my light, my guide, my way;
No foes or violence I fear,
Or fraud, while thou, my God, art near.

4 When floods my spirit overflow,
And I shall sink in waves of wo,
O, then thy timely aid impart,
To raise my head, and cheer my heart.

7.   S. M.

1 In expectation sweet,
   We wait, and sing, and pray,
Till Christ's triumphal car we meet,
   And see an endless day.

2 He comes, the Conqueror comes;
   Death falls beneath his sword;
The joyful prisoners burst the tombs,
   And rise to meet their Lord.

3 The trumpet sounds, "Awake!
   Ye dead, to judgment come!"
The pillars of creation shake,
   While man receives his doom.

4 Thrice happy morn for those
   Who love the ways of peace;
No night of sorrow ere shall close,
   Or shade their perfect bliss.

8. L. M.

1 Broad is the road that leads to death,
   And thousands walk together there;
But wisdom shows a narrow path,
   With here and there a traveller.

2 "Deny thyself and take thy cross,"
   Is the Redeemer's great command;
Nature must count her gold but dross,
   That we may gain the heavenly land.

3 The fearful soul that tires and faints,
   And walks the ways of God no more,
Is but esteemed almost a saint,
   And makes his own destruction sure.

4 Lord, let not all my hopes be vain;
   Create my heart entirely new—
Which hypocrites cannot attain,
   And vile apostates never knew.

9. P. M.

1 There is a King of glory,
   Ere long on earth to rise,
Sung in prophetic story,
   Descending from the skies;
The babe of Bethlehem is he,
   It is the man of Calvary;
Not crowned with thorns and gory,
   But crowned with glory now:

Not set at naught to-day,
Not mocked and led away,
But crowned with everlasting glory now.

2 He cometh, cometh speedy
  To save his suffering saints—
Saints groaning, waiting, ready,
  And endeth their complaints.
With joy they meet him in the air,
And shout the swelling triumph there:
No longer poor and needy,
But crowned with glory now:
  Not one reviled that day!
  None stumble in the way,
All crowned with everlasting glory now.

3 O, tears, and sin, and sighing,
  Now let your prisoners go;
Discharged from pain and dying,
  And from a world of wo!
I go to Christ, he comes to me,
We meet in bright eternity:
On clouds he cometh flying,
On clouds of glory now;
  Victorious in his wars,
  Full many a palm he bears,
And crowns of everlasting glory now.

4 O, what is tribulation—
  What all the ills I bear—
Compared with this salvation
  And all the glory there?
Behold the city fair and high,
Bright capital of earth and sky,
That dureth with duration,
All filled with glory now!
  The armies of his grace
  Triumphant reach the place:
All glory, everlasting glory now!

5 There every sight that pleases,
  There every sound that cheers,

There sweet immortal breezes,
  Inspire the palmy years;
There all the just join in one band,
From every age, from every land,
All honoring King Jesus—
All crowned with glory now:
  The people of his grace
  Have reached the heavenly place.
Hail, glory! everlasting glory now!

10. P. M.

1 Hark! the song of jubilee,
    Loud as mighty thunders roar,
  Or the fulness of the sea
    When it breaks upon the shore.

2 Hallelujah! for the Lord
    God Omnipotent shall reign;
  Hallelujah! let the word
    Echo round the earth and main.

3 Hallelujah! hark! the sound
    From the centre through the skies,
  Wakes above, beneath, around,
    All creation's harmonies.

4 See Jehovah's banner furled,
    Sheathed his sword—the work is done;
  Now the kingdoms of this world
    Are the kingdoms of his Son!

5 He shall reign from pole to pole,
    With illimitable sway;
  The wide earth he shall control;
    Nor his kingdom pass away.

11. P. M.

1 Watchman! tell us of the night,
    What its signs of promise are.
  Traveller! in yon heavenly height
    See that glory-beaming star!

Watchman! does its beauteous ray
  Aught of hope or joy foretell?
Traveller! yes, it brings the day,
  Promised day of Israel.

2 Watchman! tell us of the night;
  Higher yet that star ascends.
Traveller! blessedness and light,
  Peace and truth its course portends.
Watchman! will its beams alone,
  Gild the spot that gave them birth?
Traveller! ages are its own;
  See, it shines through all the earth!

3 Watchman! tell us of the night,
  For the morning seems to dawn.
Traveller! darkness takes its flight;
  Doubt and terror are withdrawn,
Watchman! let thy wandering cease;
  Hie thee to thy quiet home,
Traveller! lo, the Prince of peace—
  Lo, the Son of God has come!

12. P. M.

1 O thou, in whose presence my soul takes delight;
  On whom in affliction I call;
My comfort by day, and my song in the night,
  My hope, my salvation, my all;

2 O, why should I wander an alien from thee?
  Why leave my beloved and die?
Thy foes will rejoice when my sorrows they see,
  Nor heed when for pity I cry.

3 This is my Beloved, his form is divine,
  His vestments shed odors around;
The locks on his head are as grapes on the vine,
  When autumn with plenty is crowned.

4 His voice as the sound of the dulcimer sweet,
  Is heard through the shadow of death;

The cedars of Lebanon bow at his feet;
　The air is perfumed with his breath.

5 Love sits on his eyelids and scatters delight
　　Through all the bright mansions on high;
　Their faces the cherubim veil in his sight,
　　And prostrate before him they lie.

6 He looks, and the angels in glory rejoice,
　　And myriads wait for his word;
　He speaks, and eternity filled with his voice,
　　Re-echoes the praise of the Lord.

13.   P. M.

1 Hark! whence that voice?
　Hark! hear the joyful shouting!
　See, see what splendor
　Spreads its beams around us,
　　Turning dark midnight
　　Into noontide glory,
　　As it approaches.

2 With pomp majestic,
　See the heavenly vision
　Swiftly descending,
　While attending angels,
　　Pour acclamation,
　　And celestial chanting,
　　Waking attention.

3 Give God the glory,
　All ye hosts celestial;
　Peace dwells on earth,
　And man enjoys the favor!
　　Rise now, ye fallen,
　　Heirs to life eternal!
　　Through the Mediator.

4 O, may impressions
　Of God's boundless mercy,
　Ever remind us,
　Of our grateful duty:

Sweet the employment,
To proclaim his goodness
And sing his praises.

14.   L. M.

1 God, in the gospel of his Son,
Makes his eternal counsels known:
Lo, here his richest mercy shines,
And truth is drawn in fairest lines.

2 Wisdom its dictates here imparts,
To form our minds and cheer our hearts;
Its influence makes the sinner live;
It bids the drooping saint revive.

3 Our raging passions it controls,
And comfort yields to contrite souls;
It brings a better world in view,
And guides us all our journey through.

4 May this blest treasure ever lie
Close to my heart, and near my eye;
And every hour my soul engage,
And be my lasting heritage.

15.   L. M.

1 Before Jehovah's awful throne,
  Ye nations bow with sacred joy;
Know that the Lord is God alone;
  He can create, and he destroy.

2 His sovereign power, without our aid,
  Formed us of clay when we began;
And when like wandering sheep we strayed,
  He brought us to his fold again,

3 Now crowd his gates with thankful songs;
  High as the heavens your voices raise;
Let earth with her unnumbered tongues,
  Fill all his courts with sounding praise!

4 Be thou exalted, O my God,
    Above the heavens where angels dwell
Thy power on earth be known abroad,
    And land to land thy wonders tell!

16.

1 Lord, in thy temple, thou shalt hear
    My voice ascending high;
To thee will I direct my prayer;
    To thee lift up mine eye;

2 Up to that world where Christ is gone
    To plead for all his saints,
Presenting at his Father's throne
    Our songs and our complaints.

3 Thou art a God before whose sight
    The wicked shall not stand;
Sinners cannot be thy delight,
    Or dwell at thy right hand.

4 But to thy house will I resort,
    To taste thy mercies here;
I will frequent thy holy court,
    And worship in thy fear.

17.

1 To-day the Saviour calls!
    Ye wanderers come!
O ye benighted souls,
    Why longer roam?

2 To-day the Saviour calls!
    O hear him now!
Within these sacred walls
    To Jesus bow.

3 To-day the Saviour calls!
    For refuge fly;
The storm of justice falls;
    Ruin is nigh.

4 The Spirit calls to-day!
  Yield to his power;
O grieve him not away!
  This is his hour!

18.   P. M.

1 Come, ye sinners, poor and wretched,
  This is your accepted hour;
Jesus ready stands to save you,
  Full of pity, love, and power.

2 Come, ye weary, heavy-laden,
  Lost and ruined by the fall;
If you tarry till you are better,
  You will never come at all.

3 Let not conscience make you linger,
  Nor of fitness fondly dream;
All the fitness he requireth
  Is to feel your need of him.

4 O, embrace the news of pardon
  Offered to you by the Lord;
Hear his pleadings—O, how tender!
  Listen to his loving word.

19.   L. M.

1 Show pity, Lord; O Lord, forgive—
Let a repenting rebel live;
Are not thy mercies large and free?
May not a sinner trust in thee?

2 My crimes, though great, cannot surpass
The power and glory of thy grace;
Great God, thy nature hath no bound;
So let thy pardoning love be found.

3 O, wash my soul from every sin,
And make my guilty conscience clean!
Here, on my heart, the burden lies,
And past offences pain mine eyes.

4 O, save a trembling sinner, Lord,
   Whose hope is hovering round thy word,
   To light on some sweet promise there,
   Some sure support against despair.

20.   P. M.

1 In Eden's bowers so lovely,
    Where oft we yet shall stray,
  Where fountains sweet are gushing,
    Shines one eternal day,
  Shines one eternal day—
    Never forget will I—
  And for Jesus Christ my Saviour,
    I would lay me down and die.

2 There gentle breezes ever
    Will fan the victor's brow;
  There songs of heavenly concert,
    Fill the ever present now,
  Fill the ever present now—
    To be there still I cry;
  And for Jesus Christ my Saviour,
    I would lay me down and die.

3 There the trees of life are growing
    In the Paradise of God;
  There the stream of life is flowing
    In the midst of that abode,
  In the midst of that abode—
    To be there I will try,
  And for Jesus Christ my Saviour,
    I would lay me down and die.

4 There is pleasure, never dying,
    At thy right hand, O Lord!
  There by the holy angels
    Our Jesus is adored,
  Our Jesus is adored—
    He sits enthroned on high.
  Glory unto Christ the Saviour,
    Who for us came down to die.

21. P. M.

1 O, how happy are they
  Who their Saviour obey,
And have laid up their treasure above!
  Tongue can never express
  The sweet comfort and peace
Of a soul in its earliest love.

2 That sweet comfort was mine
  When the favor divine
I first found in the blood of the Lamb;
  When, at first, I believed
  What a joy I received!
What a heaven in Jesus' blest name!

3 Jesus all the day long
  Was my joy and my song;
O that all his salvation might see!
  He hath loved me, I cried,
  He hath suffered and died,
To redeem even rebels like me.

4 O the rapturous height
  Of that holy delight
Which I felt in the life-giving blood!
  Of my Saviour possessed,
  I was perfectly blest,
As if filled with the fulness of God!

22. C. M.

1 Father of mercies, in thy word
  What endless glory shines!
Forever be thy name adored
  For these immortal lines.

2 Here the blest tree of knowledge grows,
  And yields a rich repast;
Here purer sweets than nature knows
  Invite the longing taste.

3 Lo, here the Saviour's welcome voice
　　Spreads heavenly peace around;
　And life, and everlasting joys
　　Attend the blissful sound.

4 O may this heavenly treasure be
　　My ever-dear delight;
　And still new beauties may I see,
　　And still increasing light.

23.   C. M.

1 What shall I render to my God
　　For all his kindness shown?
　My feet shall visit thine abode,
　　My songs address thy throne.

2 Among the saints who fill thy house,
　　My offerings shall be paid;
　There shall my zeal perform the vows
　　My soul in anguish made.

3 How happy all thy servants are!
　　How great thy grace to me!
　My life, which thou hast made thy care,
　　Lord, I devote to thee.

4 Now I am thine, forever thine,
　　Nor shall my purpose move;
　Thy hand hath loosed my bonds of pain,
　　And bound me with thy love!

24.   C. M.

1 Thine oath and promise, mighty God,
　　Recorded in thy word,
　Become our hope's foundation broad,
　　And surety afford.

2 Like Abraham, the friend of God,
　　Thy faithfulness we prove;
　We tread in paths the fathers trod,
　　Blest with thy light and love.

3 Largely our consolation flows,
   While we expect the day
That ends our griefs, and pains, and woes,
   And drives our fears away.

4 Let floods of mighty vengeance roll,
   And compass earth around;
Let thunder sound from pole to pole,
   And earthquakes vast astound;

5 Let nature all convulse and shake,
   And angry nations rage;
Thy name our hiding-place we make:
   To save thou dost engage.

25.   L. M.

1 When marshalled on the nightly plain,
   The glittering host bestud the sky,
One star alone of all the train,
   Can fix the sinner's wandering eye.

2 Hark! Hark! to God the chorus breaks
   From every host, from every gem;
But one alone the Saviour speaks,—
   It is the star of Bethlehem.

3 Once on the raging seas I rode;
   The storm was loud, the night was dark;
The ocean yawned, and rudely blowed
   The wind that tossed my foundering bark.

4 Deep horror then my courage froze;
   Death-struck, I ceased the tide to stem;
When suddenly a star arose,—
   It was the star of Bethlehem.

5 It was my guide, my light, my all;
   It bade my dark foreboding cease;
And through the storm and danger's thrall,
   It led me to the port of peace.

6 Now, safely moored from perils sore,
   I sing first in night's diadem,
Most joyfully forevermore,
   The brilliant star of Bethlehem.

26.   C. M.

1 There is a fountain filled with blood,
   Drawn from Immanuel's veins;
And sinners plunged beneath that flood,
   Lose all their guilty stains.

2 The dying thief rejoiced to see
   That fountain in his day;
And there may I, though vile as he,
   Wash all my sins away.

3 Dear dying Lamb, thy precious blood
   Shall never lose its power,
Till all the ransomed church of God
   Be saved, to sin no more.

4 And since, by faith, I saw the stream
   Thy flowing wounds supply,
Redeeming love has been my theme,
   And shall be till I die.

5 I, in a nobler sweeter song,
   Shall sing thy power to save,
When this poor lisping stammering tongue
   Is ransomed from the grave.

27.   S. M.

1 Beside the gospel pool,
   Appointed for the poor,
From day to day my helpless soul
   Hath waited for a cure.

2 How often have I thought,
   Why should I longer lie?
Surely the mercy I have sought
   Is not for such as I.

3 But whither can I go?
    There is no other pool
Where streams of sovereign mercy flow
    To make a sinner whole.

4 Still, then from day to day
    I wait, and hope, and try.
Can Jesus hear a sinner pray,
    Yet suffer him to die?

28.   L. M.

1 The Christian warrior, see him stand,
    In the whole armor of his God;
The Spirit's sword is in his hand;
    His feet are with the gospel shod.

2 In panoply of truth complete,
    Salvation's helmet on his head,
With righteousness, a breastplate meet,
    And faith's broad shield before him spread.

3 With this omnipotence he moves;
    From this the rebel armies flee;
Till more than conqueror he proves,
    Through Christ, who gives him victory.

4 Thus strong in his Redeemer's Strength,
    Sin, death, and hell he tramples down;
Fights the good fight, and wins at length,
    Through mercy, an immortal crown.

29.   L. M.

1 Wait on the Lord, ye heirs of hope,
    And let his word support each soul;
Well can he bear your courage up,
    And all your foes and fears control.

2 He waits his own well chosen hour,
    Intended mercy to display;
Oft his paternal pity moves,
    While wisdom dictates a delay.

3 Blest are the patient souls that wait
    With sweet submission to his will;
Harmonious all their passions move,
    And in the midst of storms are still.

4 And when their Father's well known voice
    Wakens their silence into songs,
Then earth grows vocal with his praise,
    And heaven the grateful shout prolongs.

30.   L. M.

1 Stand up, my soul, shake off thy fears,
    And gird the gospel armor on;
March to the gates of endless joy,
    Where Jesus has before thee gone,

2 Hell and thy sins resist thy course;
    But hell and sin are vanquished foes;
Thy Saviour nailed them to the cross,
    And sung the triumph when he rose.

3 Then let my soul march boldly on,
    Press forward to the heavenly gate;
There peace and joy eternal reign,
    And glittering robes for conquerors wait.

4 There shall I wear the victor's crown,
    And magnify almighty grace;
While all the armies of the skies
    Join in my glorious Leader's praise.

31.   C. M.

1 When I can read my title clear
    To mansions in the skies,
I bid farewell to every fear,
    And wipe my weeping eyes.

2 Let earth against my soul engage,
    And fiery darts be hurled,
Then I can smile at Satan's rage,
    And face a frowning world.

3 Let cares like a wild deluge come,
   Let storms of sorrow fall;
  So I but safely reach my home,
   My God, my rest, my all.

4 There happier bowers than Eden's bloom,
   Nor sin nor sorrow know;
  Blest fields, through rude and stormy scenes
   I onward press to you.

32.   S. M.

1 Equip me for the war,
   And teach me, Lord, to fight;
  My heart with fervency prepare,
   And guide me ever right.

2 Control my every thought;
   My whole of sin remove;
  Let all my works in thee be wrought;
   Let all be wrought in love.

3 O, arm me with the mind,
   Meek Lamb, that was in thee,
  And let my knowing zeal be joined,
   With perfect charity.

4 O, may I love like thee,
   In all thy footsteps tread!
  Forever hate iniquity,
   But nothing thou hast made.

33.   C. M.

1 Am I a soldier of the cross,
   A follower of the Lamb?
  And shall I fear to own his cause,
   Or blush to speak his name!

2 Sure I must fight if I would reign;
   Increase my courage, Lord,
  To bear the toil, endure the pain,
   Supported by thy word.

3 Thy saints in all this glorious war
   Shall conquer, though they die;
   They see the triumph from afar
   By faith's discerning eye.

4 When that illustrious day shall rise,
   And all thine armies shine,
   In robes of victory through the skies,
   The glory shall be thine.

34.   P. M.

1 Soldiers of the cross, arise!
   Lo, your Leader, from the skies,
   Waves before you glory's prize—
     Prize of victory.
   Seize your armor, gird it on;
   Lo, the strife will soon be done;
   Soon the battle will be won;
     Struggle manfully.

2 Jesus conquered when he fell!
   Met and vanquished earth and hell;
   Now he leads you on to swell
     The triumphs of his cross.
   Though all earth and hell appear,
   Who will doubt, or who will fear?
   God our strength and shield is near;
     We shall gain our cause.

3 Onward, then, ye hosts of God!
   Jesus points the victor's road;
   Follow where your Leader trod;
     You shall see his face.
   Soon your foes shall all be slain;
   Crowns of glory you shall gain,
   When you with the conquering train,
     Shout your Leader's praise.

35.   P. M.

1 Come let us anew
  Our journey pursue,
Roll round with the year,
And never stand still
  Till the Master appear.

2 His adorable will
  Let us gladly fulfil,
And our talents improve,
By the patience of hope,
  And the labor of love.

3 Our life as a dream,
  Our time as a stream,
Glides swiftly away;
And the fugitive moment
  Refuses to stay.

4 O that each in the day
  Of his coming may say,
"I have fought my way through;
I have finished the work
  Thou didst give me to do."

36.   P. M.

1 Jesus, at thy command
  I launch into the deep,
And leave my native land,
  Where sin lulls all asleep;
For thee I fain would all resign,
And thus embark with thee and thine.

2 Christ is my pilot wise,
  My compass is his word;
My soul each storm defies
  While I have such a Lord;
I trust his faithfulness and power,
To save me in the trying hour.

3 Though rocks and quicksands deep
   Through all my passage lie,
  Yet he shall safely keep
   And guide me with his eye:
How can I sink with such a prop,
That bears the world and all things up.

4 By faith I see the land,
   The port of endless rest;
  O, make my sails expand,
   My Saviour, ever blest!
O, may I reach the heavenly shore,
Where winds and waves distress no more!

37.   C. M.

1 In evil long I took delight,
   Unawed by shame or fear,
  Till a new object struck my sight,
   And checked my wild career.

2 I saw one hanging on a tree,
   In agonies and blood,
  Who fixed his languid eyes on me,
   As near his cross I stood.

3 Sure never till my latest breath
   Can I forget that look;
  It seemed to charge me with his death,
   Though not a word he spoke.

4 A second look he gave, which said,
   "I freely all forgive;
  This blood is for your ransom paid;
   I die that you may live."

38.   C. M.

1 O, for a faith that will not shrink,
   Though pressed by many a foe;
  That will not tremble on the brink
   Of poverty or wo.

2 A faith that shines more bright and clear
  When tempests rage without;
That when in danger knows no fear,
  In darkness feels no doubt.

3 That bears unmoved the world's dread frown,
  Nor heeds its scornful smile;
That sin's wild ocean cannot drown,
  Nor its soft arts beguile;

4 A faith that keeps the narrow way,
  By truth restrained and led,
And with a pure and heavenly ray
  Lights up the dying bed,

39. C. M.

1 Amazing grace! how sweet the sound!
  That saved a wretch like me;
I once was lost, but now am found;
  Was blind, but now I see.

2 Thy grace has taught me, Lord, to fear,
  And grace my fears relieved;
How precious did thy grace appear
  The hour I first believed!

3 Through many dangers, toils, and snares,
  I have already come;
Thy grace has led me safe thus far,
  And grace shall lead me home.

4 The Lord has promised good to me;
  His word my hope secures;
He will my shield and portion be
  As long as life endures.

5 And when these mortal powers shall fail,
  And present life shall cease,
I shall possess, within the veil,
  A life of joy and peace.

6 Then let the earth dissolve like snow,
   And pass the years of time,
That God, who led me here below,
   Will be forever mine.

40. L. M.

1 High in the heavens, eternal God,
   Thy goodness in full glory shines;
Thy truth shall break through every cloud
   That veils and darkens thy designs.

2 Forever firm thy justice stands,
   As mountains their foundations keep;
Wise are the wonders of thy hands;
   Thy judgments are a mighty deep.

3 Thy providence is kind and large;
   Both man and beast thy bounty share;
The whole creation is thy charge,
   But saints are thy peculiar care.

4 My God! how excellent thy grace,
   Whence all our hope and comfort springs!
The sons of Adam in distress
   Fly to the shadow of thy wings.

41. L. M.

1 Kingdoms and thrones to God belong;
Crown him, ye nations, in your song;
His wondrous name and power rehearse;
His honors shall enrich your verse.

2 He rides and thunders through the sky;
His name, Jehovah, sounds on high;
Sing to his name, ye chosen race;
Rejoice, ye saints before his face.

3 He breaks the captive's heavy chain,
   And prisoners see the light again;
But rebels who dispute his will,
   Shall dwell in gloomy darkness still.

4 Proclaim him King, pronounce him blest;
He is your fountain and your rest;
When terrors rise, and nations faint,
God is the strength of every saint.

42. S. M.

1 How perfect is thy word!
　Thy judgments all are just;
And ever in thy promise, Lord,
　May we securely trust.

2 I hear thy word in love;
　In faith thy word obey;
O, send thy Spirit from above,
　And teach me, Lord, thy way.

3 Thy counsels all are plain,
　Thy precepts all are pure;
Eternal as thy years remain
　So shall thy truth endure.

4 O, may my soul with joy,
　Trust in thy faithful word;
Be it through life my glad employ
　To keep thy precepts, Lord.

43. L. M.

1 Jehovah reigns! he dwells in light,
Girded with majesty and might;
The world, created by his hands,
Still on its firm foundation stands.

2 But ere this spacious world was made,
Or had its first foundation laid,
Thy throne eternal ages stood,
Thyself the ever-living God!

3 Like floods the angry nations rise,
And aim their rage against the skies;
In vain their rage they aim so high!
At thy rebuke the billows die.

4 For ever shall thy throne endure;
Thy promise stands for ever sure;
And everlasting holiness
Becomes the dwellings of thy grace.

44.   P. M.

1 Lo, he comes, with clouds descending,
Once for favored sinners slain!
Thousand, thousand saints attending,
Swell the triumph of his train.
Hallelujah!
Jesus comes on earth to reign!

2 Every eye shall now behold him,
Robed in dreadful majesty;
Those who set at naught and sold him,
Pierced and nailed him to the tree,
Deeply wailing,
Shall the true Messiah see.

3 When the solemn trump has sounded,
Heaven and earth shall flee away.
All who hate him must, confounded,
Hear the summons of that day:
"Come to judgment!
Come to judgment, come away!"

45.   P. M.

1 In the sun, and moon, and stars,
Signs and wonders there shall be;
Earth shall quake with fearful wars,
Nations with perplexity.

2 On the ocean's hoary deep
Stronger tempests shall arise;
Darker storms the mountains sweep,
Fiercer lightnings rend the skies.

3 Evil thoughts shall shake the proud,
Racking doubt and restless fear;

And, amid the blazing cloud,
  Shall the Judge of men appear.

4 But, though from that awful face,
  Heaven shall fade and earth shall fly,
Fear not ye, his chosen race,
  Your redemption then is nigh.

46.

1 My soul is happy when I hear
  The Saviour is so nigh;
I long to see his sign appear
  Upon the parting sky.

2 I love to wait, and watch, and pray,
  And trust his living word,
And feel the coming of that day
  No longer is deferred.

3 I do rejoice that life is given
  In these last days to me,
That deathless I may rise to heaven,
  And my Redeemer see.

4 Then, waiting brethren, let us sing—
  He will not tarry long—
And fill with love the hours that bring
  The glory of our song.

5 Yes, he will come, no longer fear,
  Though earth and hell assail;
His word attests the moment near,
  And that can never fail.

47.

1 The glorious day is coming,
  The hour is rolling on,
Its radiant light is beaming,
  Resplendent as the sun;

In yon bright clouds of heaven
  The Saviour will appear,
And gather all his chosen
  To meet him in the air.

2 Then fire from God descending,
  Shall sweep from shore to shore,
And nations, loud lamenting,
  Shall sink to rise no more.
Though tears with groans are blended,
  Yet vainly now they cry;
The day of hope is ended,
  And sinners all must die.

3 But saints shall be victorious,
  And joy to meet the Lord;
An earth more bright and glorious
  Is promised in his word.
Our God himself, there reigning,
  Shall wipe all tears away;
No darkness then remaining,
  But one eternal day.

4 O, Christian, wake from sleeping,
  And let your works abound;
Be watching, praying, weeping,
  For soon the trump will sound!
O, sinner, hear the warning;
  To Jesus quickly fly;
Then you, on that blest morning,
  May meet him in the sky.

48.

1 From whence doth this union arise,
  That hatred is conquered by love?
It fastens our souls in such ties
  That nothing prevails to remove.

2 Why are we unwilling to part,
  Since we shall ere long meet again?
Engraved on Immanuel's heart,
  At distance we cannot remain.

3 And when we shall see the glad day,
   When Jesus descends from above,
  And glory and power display,
   We then to his kingdom remove.

4 With Jesus we ever shall reign,
   And all his bright beauty shall see,
  And sing, Hallelujah, amen!
   Amen, even so let it be!

49. C. M.

1 On Jordan's stormy bank I stand,
   And cast a wishful eye
  To Canaan's fair and happy land,
   Where my possessions lie.

2 O, the transporting rapturous scene
   That rises to my sight!
  Sweet fields arrayed in living green,
   And rivers of delight.

3 There generous fruits, that never fail,
   On trees immortal grow;
  There rock, and hill, and brook, and vale,
   With milk and honey flow.

4 On all those wide, extended plains,
   Shines one eternal day;
  There God in light forever reigns,
   And scatters night away.

50. P. M.

1 There is a land of calm delight,
   To sorrowing mortals given;
  Where rapturous scenes enchant the sight,
  And all to sooth their souls unite;
   It is the gift of heaven.

2 There glory shines on all the plains,
   And joy for hope is given;
  There music swells in sweetest strains,

And spotless beauty ever reigns;
　　It is the gift of heaven.

3 There cloudless skies are ever bright;
　　Thence gloomy scenes are driven;
　There, falling on the ravished sight,
　Forever beams unsullied light;
　　It is the gift of heaven.

4 There is a stream ever to flow,
　　To ransomed pilgrims given;
　There fairest fruits, immortal grow,
　And fadeless flowers forever blow;
　　It is the gift of heaven.

51.

1 Will you go, sinner, go
　　To the high lands of Eden?
　Where no storms ever blow;
　　Where all bright days are given;
　Where the sweet, blooming flowers
　　Are their odors emitting,
　And the leaves of the bowers
　　In the breezes are flitting.

2 There the saints, robed in white,
　　Sing by life's flowing fountains;
　Shining beauteous and bright,
　　Lo, they shout from the mountains.
　There no sin, or dismay,
　　Neither trouble or sorrow,
　Will be known for the day,
　　Or be feared for the morrow.

3 Christ prepares thee a home—
　　Sinner, canst thou believe it?
　And invites thee to come—
　　Sinner, wilt thou receive it?
　O come, sinner, come,
　　For life's tide is receding,
　And the Saviour will soon,
　　And forever cease pleading.

52.　　　　C. M.

1 What heavenly music do I hear?
　　Salvation sounding free!
　Ye souls in bondage, lend an ear,
　　And hail the Jubilee!

2 How sweetly do the tidings roll
　　All round from sea to sea,
　From land to land, from pole to pole!
　　All hail the Jubilee!

3 Jesus is on the mercy-seat;
　　Before him bend the knee;
　Let heaven and earth his praise repeat,
　　And hail the Jubilee!

4 Sinners, be wise, return and come
　　Unto the Saviour free;
　The gospel bids you welcome home,
　　To hail the Jubilee!

53.　　　　P. M.

When shall the voice of singing
　Flow joyfully along?
When hill and valley, ringing
　With one triumphant song,
Proclaim the contest ended,
　And he who once was slain,
Again to earth descended,
　In righteousness to reign.

54.　　　　P. M.

1 Away with our sorrow and fear!
　　We soon shall recover our home;
　The city of God shall appear;
　　The day of eternity come.

2 Then mourning shall be at an end,
　　When, raised by the life-giving word,
　We see the new city descend,
　　Adorned as a bride for her Lord.

3 By faith we already behold
   That holy Jerusalem here!
With buildings of jasper and gold,
   And light as the crystal so clear.

4 There saints in God's presence receive
   Their great and eternal reward;
With Jesus forever they live,
   And reign on the earth with their Lord.

55.   P. M.

1 The last lovely morning, all blooming and fair,
Is fast onward fleeting, and soon will appear.

CHORUS.
While the mighty, mighty, mighty trump
Sounds, "Come, come away!"
O, let us be ready to hail the glad day.

2 The Bridegroom from glory to earth shall descend;
And thousands of angels around him attend.

3 The graves will be opened, the dead will arise,
And with their Redeemer will meet in the skies.

4 The saints, then immortal, in glory shall reign,
The bride with the Bridegroom for ever remain.

56.   C. M.

1 When the last trumpet's awful voice
   This rolling earth shall shake;
Then opening graves shall yield their charge,
   And dust to life awake.

2 Those bodies that corrupted fell
   Shall incorrupted rise;
And mortal forms shall spring to life
   Immortal in the skies.

3 Behold, what heavenly prophets sung
   Shall be, at last, fulfilled:

That Death shall yield his ancient reign,
   And vanquished quit the field.

4 Let Faith exalt her joyful voice,
   And thus begin to sing:
   "O Grave, where is thy victory now?
   And where, O Death, thy sting?"

57. P. M.

1 The voice of free grace cries, "Escape to the mountain;
For Adam's lost race Christ has opened a fountain;
For sin and uncleanness—for every transgression—
His blood flows most freely in streams of salvation."

CHORUS.

Hallelujah! to the Lamb, who has purchased our pardon,
We will praise him again when we pass over Jordan!

2 O, Jesus, ride on, thy triumphs are glorious,
Over sin, death and hell, to make us victorious:
Thy name shall be praised in the great congregation,
And saints shall delight to ascribe thee salvation.

3 When immortal we stand, having gained the blest shore,
With our harps in our hands, we will praise him evermore:
We will range the bright fields on the banks of the river,
And sing hallelujahs for ever and ever!

58. C. M.

1 With joy we meditate the grace
   Of our High Priest above;
   His spirit yearns with tenderness,
   And everlasting love.

2 Touched with a sympathy within,
   He knows our feeble frame;

He knows what sore temptations mean,
   For he has felt the same.

3 He, in the days of mortal flesh,
   Poured out his prayers and tears;
And now in glory feels afresh
   What every member bears.

4 He will not quench the smoking flax,
   But raise it to a flame;
The bruised reed he never breaks,
   Or scorns the meanest name,

59.   C. M.

1 The Lord our God is clothed with might;
   All nature owns his will;
He speaks, and in his heavenly height
   The rolling sun stands still.

2 Let waves rebel, and on the land
   With threatening aspect roar!
The Lord lifts up his awful hand,
   And chains them to the shore.

3 Let stormy winds their force combine;
   Without his high behest
They shall not, in the mountain pine,
   Disturb the sparrow's nest.

4 His voice sublime is heard afar;
   In thunder peals it flies;
He binds the whirlwind to his car;
   And sweeps the howling skies.

5 Ye nations bend—with reverence bend;
   Ye monarchs wait his nod,
And bid your highest songs ascend
   To celebrate our God.

60. P. M

1 Salem's great King, Jesus by name,
In ancient time to Jordan came,
All righteousness to fill;
And there the waiting Baptist stood.
Whose name was John, a man of God,
To do his Master's will.

2 Down in old Jordan's rolling flood,
The Baptist led the Lamb of God,
And there did him baptize;
Jehovah saw his darling Son,
And was well pleased with what was done,
And owned him from the skies.

3 "This is my Son," Jehovah cries:
On him to rest the Spirit flies:
O, children, hear ye him.
Hark! hear his voice; behold, he cries,
"Repent, believe, and be baptized,
And wash away your sin."

4 Come, children, come, his voice obey:
Salem's great King has marked the way,
And has a crown prepared;
O then arise and give consent,
Walk in the way that Jesus went,
And have the great reward!

61. C. M.

1 O, how I long to see that day
When the redeemed shall come
To Zion clad in white array—
Their blissful, endless home!

CHORUS.

O, carry me home, carry me home
To Mount Zion;
O, carry me home to that world of light,
Where all the saints shall dwell.

2 My longing heart cries out. O, come!
   Creation groans for thee!
   O, come, and bring thy people home—
   Bring immortality.

62.   P. M.

1 On the mountain's top appearing,
   Lo, the sacred herald stands.
  Welcome news to Zion bearing,
   Zion long in hostile lands;
     Mourning captive,
   God himself will loose thy bands.

2 Has thy night been long and mournful?
   Have thy friends unfaithful proved?
  Have thy foes been proud and scornful,
   By thy sighs and tears unmoved?
     Cease thy mourning:
   Zion still is well beloved.

3 God, thy God, will now restore thee,
   He himself appears thy friend;
  All thy foes shall flee before thee;
   Here their boasts and triumphs end:
     Great deliverance
   Zion's King will surely send.

63.   P. M.

1 How happy are the little flock,
  Who, safe beneath their guardian Rock,
   In all commotions rest!
  When war's and tumult's waves run high,
  Unmoved above the storm they lie,
   And lodge in Jesus' breast.

2 Such happiness, O Lord, have we,
  By mercy gathered into thee,
   Before the floods descend;
  And while the bursting cloud comes down,
  We mark the vengeful day begun,
   And calmly wait the end.

3 Thy tokens we with joy confess;
   The war proclaims thee Prince of Peace;
   The earthquake speaks thy power;
   The famine all thy fulness brings;
   The plague presents thy healing wings
   In nature's final hour.

4 Whatever ills the world befall,
   A pledge of endless good we call,
   A sign of Jesus near;
   His chariot will not long delay;
   We hear the rumbling wheels, and pray,
   "Triumphant Lord, appear!"

64. P. M.

1 We have heard from the bright, the better land;
   We have heard, and our hearts are glad;
   For we were a lonely, pilgrim band,
   And weary, and worn, and sad.
   They tell us the pilgrims ever dwell there—
   No longer are homeless ones.
   We know that goodly land is fair;
   Life's river of water there runs.

2 We hear that the fields are waving there
   With a rich and abundant show,
   That the mountains and the vales afar
   All in blooming beauty glow;
   And lovely birds in the bowers green
   Their melody ever repeat,
   And music mingles in every scene
   From the harpings of angels, most sweet.

3 We have heard of the robe, the palm, the crown,
   And the rapturous band in white;
   Of the city of gems in high renown,
   Illumined with heavenly light;
   The King is seen in his beauty rare—
   The joy and the light of the land;
   In a little while and we hope to be there,
   To sing with that glorious band.

65.

1 When shall I see the day
    That ends my woes?
  When shall I victory gain
    Over my foes?
  When will the trumpet sound
    That calls the exiles home?
  The grand Sabbatic year,
    When will it come?

2 A crown of glory bright,
    By faith I see,
  In yonder realms of light,
    Prepared for me.
  O, may I faithful prove,
    And keep the prize in view,
  And through the storms of life
    My way pursue.

3 Jesus, be thou my guide;
    My steps attend;
  O, keep me near thy side!
    Be thou my friend;
  Be thou my shield and sun.
    My Saviour and my guard;
  And, when my work is done,
    My great reward.

4 O, how I long to see
    That happy day,
  When sorrow, pain, and sin
    Shall pass away,
  When all the heavenly tribes
    Shall find their blissful home!
  The jubilee of God,
    When will it come?

66.   P. M.

1 Drooping souls, no longer grieve,
    Heaven is propitious!
If in Christ you will believe,
    You shall find him precious.
Jesus now is passing by,
    Calling mourners to him:
Drooping souls, you need not die,
    Only be believing!

2 He has pardons, full and free,
    Drooping souls to gladden;
Lo, he cries, "Come unto me,
    Weary, heavy-laden."
Though your sins, like mountains high,
    Rise, and reach to heaven!
Soon as you on him rely,
    All shall be forgiven.

3 Worthy is the Saviour's name.
    Let the world adore him;
He to save the dying came,—
    Let us bow before him:
Wandering sinners, now return:
    Contrite souls, believe him:
Drooping ones, why will you mourn,
    And be unbelieving?

67.   L. M.

1 My heavenly home is bright and fair,
No pain or death can enter there:
Its glittering towers the sun outshine;
That glorious mansion shall be mine.

CHORUS.

I am going home, I am going home,
    I am going home to die no more,
'To die no more, to die no more,
    I am going home to die no more.

2 While here, a stranger now I roam,
 Affliction's waves may round me foam;
 And though, like Lazarus, sick and poor,
 My heavenly mansion stands secure.

3 Let others seek a home below,
 Where flames devour, floods overflow;
 Be mine the happier lot to own
 A mansion nearer to the throne.

68.   L. M.

1 Together let us sweetly live,
  I am bound for the land of Canaan;
 Together let us all believe,
  I am bound for the land of Canaan.

CHORUS.

O Canaan, bright Canaan,
 I am bound for the land of Canaan;
O, Canaan it is my happy home,
 I am bound for the land of Canaan.

2 Then come with me, beloved friend,
  I am bound for the land of Canaan;
 Our future joys shall never end,
  I am bound for the land of Canaan.

69.   C. M.

1 Ye valiant soldiers of the cross,
  Ye happy, praying band,
 Though in this world you suffer loss,
  Press on to Canaan's land.

CHORUS.

Let us never mind the scoffs
Or the frowns of the world,
 For we all have the cross to bear;
It will only make the crown
The brighter to shine
 When we have the crown to wear.

2 All earthly pleasures we forsake
   When glory is in view:
   In Jesus' strength we undertake
   To fight our passage through.

70.   P. M.

1 My days are gliding swiftly by,
   And I, a pilgrim stranger,
   Would not detain them as they fly,
   Those hours of toil and danger.

Chorus.—For O! we stand on Jordan's strand,
   And soon shall all pass over,
   And just before, the shining shore
   We may almost discover.

2 We gird our loins with truth divine,
   Our distant land discerning;
   Our Lord commands our light to shine;
   Let all our lamps be burning.

3 Should coming days be dark and drear,
   We need not cease our singing;
   Our Master bids us not to fear;
   To Him our hearts are clinging.

4 Let sorrow's rudest tempest blow,
   Each cord on earth to sever,
   Our King says, "Come"—we hasten home
   To dwell with Him forever.

71.   L. M.

1 The gospel trumpet now is blown,
   That to the wanderers may be known
   The mercy of their Lord and King,
   To cause their hearts with joy to sing.

Chorus.—As we march along to glory
   We will sing salvation free;
   We will tell the joyful story
   Of the coming Jubilee.

2 When on the part of God we rise
  And take the cross, we win a prize;
  And though temptations oft prevail,
  Our songs of triumph shall not fail.

3 If we prove faithful to the end,
  We shall find Christ a constant friend;
  For he who loves us watches keeps;
  He never faints, he never sleeps.

72. P. M.

1 We are bound for the land
  Of the pure and the holy,
    The home of the happy
    Prepared from above;
  Ye wanderers from God,
  In the broad road of folly,
    O say, will you go to the Eden of love?

CHORUS.

Will you go, will you go, will you go, will you go?
O say, will you go to the Eden of Love?

2 In that blessed land,
    Neither sighing or anguish
      Can breathe in the fields
      Where the glorified rove.
  Ye heart-burdened ones,
  Who in misery languish,
    O say, will you go to the Eden of love?

73. P. M.

1 Out on an ocean most fearful we ride,
    All homeward bound, homeward bound;
  Tossed on the waves of a rough restless tide.
    All homeward bound, homeward bound;
  Far from a harbor all drear, we have rode,
  Seeking our Father's enchanting abode,
  Promise of which on us he has bestowed:
    All homeward bound, homeward bound.

2 Wildly the storm sweeps us on as it roars,
   All homeward bound, homeward bound;
Look! yonder lie the bright, heavenly shores!
   All homeward bound, homeward bound.
Steady, O pilot! stand firm at the wheel.
Steady! we soon shall outweather the gale;
O, how we fly with a loud creaking sail!
   All homeward bound, homeward bound.

3 Into the harbor at length we shall glide,
   All home at last, home at last,
Safely adrift on the bright silver tide,
   All home at last, home at last:
Glory to God! there are dangers no more!
We are secure on the glorified shore:
Glory to God! we shall shout evermore,
   All home at last, home at last.

74.   P. M.

1 Mark that pilgrim lowly bending
At the shrine of prayer; ascending
Praise and sighs together blending
   From his lips in mournful strain;
Glowing with sincere contrition,
And with child-like blest submission,
Ever riseth this petition:
   "Jesus, come, O come to reign!"

2 List again: the low earth sigheth,
For the blood of martyrs crieth
From its bosom, where there lieth
   Millions upon millions slain:
"Lord, how long ere thy word given,
All the wicked shall be driven
From the earth by bolts of heaven?
   Jesus, come, O come to reign!"

3 Kingdoms now are reeling, falling,
Nations lie in wo appalling,
On their sages vainly calling
   All these wonders to explain;

While the slain around are lying,
God's own little flock are sighing,
And in secret places crying,
  "Jesus, come, O come to reign!"

4 Here the wicked live securely,
Of to-morrow boasting surely,
While from those who walk most purely
  They extort dishonest gain:
Yea, the meek are burdened, driven,
Want and care to them are given,
But they lift the cry to heaven,
  "Jesus, come, O come to reign!"

5 Christian, cheer! the time is nearing!
Still be hopeful, nothing fearing;
Soon in majesty appearing,
  You shall hail the Lamb once slain.
O, how joyful then to hear him,
While all nations shall revere him,
Saying to his flock who fear him,
  "I have come on earth to reign!"

75.   P. M.

1 "Are we almost there, are we almost there?"
  Says the weary saint as he sighs for home.
Are those the verdant trees that rear
  Their stately forms in the high, bright dome?"

2 Then he talks of the flowers, and the clear rolling
    stream,
  That flows through the paradise of God;
And he longs to wake from life's troubled dream.
  To walk the golden street abroad.

3 He is weary and sad in this world's rude strife,
  And pants for a holy, peaceful clime;
To glow with the vigor of endless life,
  And be compassed no more by the bounds of time

4 He is waiting to hear the trumpet sound,
 And to meet his Saviour in the air!
The bright day dawns! lo, with joyous bound.
 He exclaims, "Indeed, we are almost there!"

76. P. M.

1 O God, my inmost soul convert,
 And deeply on my thoughtful heart
  Eternal things impress;
 Give me to feel their solemn weight,
 And tremble on the brink of fate,
  And wake to righteousness.

2 Before me place in dread array,
 The pomp of that tremendous day,
  When Christ with clouds shall come,
 To judge the nations at his bar;
 And tell me, Lord, shall I be there
  To meet a joyful doom?

3 Be this my one great business here,
 With serious industry and fear
  Thy favor to secure,
 Thine utmost counsel to fulfil,
 And suffer all thy righteous will,
  And to the end endure.

77. S. M.

1 Thou Judge of quick and dead,
  Before whose awful bar,
 With holy joy or guilty dread,
  We all must soon appear;

2 Our souls by grace prepare
  For that tremendous day,
 And fill us now with watchful care,
  And stir us up to pray.

3 To pray and wait the hour,
  That awful hour unknown,
 When, robed in majesty and power,
  Thou shalt from heaven come down;

4 The mighty Son of man,
   To judge the human race,
  With all thy Father's dazzling train,
   With all thy glorious grace.

78.   P. M.

1 Hail to the brightness of Zion's glad morning!
   Joy to the lands that in darkness have lain!
  Hushed be the accents of sorrow and mourning;
   Zion in triumph begins her mild reign.

2 Hail to the brightness of Zion's glad morning,
   Long by the prophets of Israel foretold!
  Hail to the millions from bondage returning!
   Gentiles and Jews the blest vision behold.

3 Lo, in the desert rich flowers are springing;
   Streams ever copious are gliding along;
  Loud from the mountain-tops echoes are ringing;
   Wastes rise in verdure and mingle in song.

4 See the dead risen from land and from ocean!
   Praise to Jehovah ascendeth on high;
  Fallen the engines of war and commotion!
   Shouts of salvation are rending the sky!

79.   P. M.

1 We are going home, led by visions bright
Of that holy land, that world of light,
Where the long, dark night of time is past,
And the morn of glory has come at last;
Where the weary saint no more shall roam,
But dwell in a sunny, peaceful home;
Where the brow with immortal gems is crowned,
And the waves of light are rolling around.

CHORUS.

O, that beautiful world! O, that beautiful world!

2 We are going home, we soon shall be
Where the sky is clear and the soil is free;
Where the victor's song floats over the plains.
And the seraph's anthems blend with its strains:
Where the sun rolls down its brilliant flood,
And beams on a world that is fair and good;
And stars, that dimmed at nature's doom,
Will sparkle and shine on the new earth's bloom.

3 Where the tears and sighs which here were given
Are exchanged for the gladsome song of heaven:
Where the beauteous forms which sing and shine
Are guarded well by a hand divine.
Pure love's banner and friendship's wand
Are waving above that princely band,
And the glory of God, like a molten sea,
Will bathe that immortal company.

4 Mid the ransomed throng, mid the sea of bliss.
Mid the holy city's gorgeousness,
Mid the verdant plains, mid angels' cheer,
Mid the flowers that never of winter wear;
Where the conqueror's song, as it sounds afar.
Is wafted on the ambrosial air;
Through endless years we there shall prove
The depth of a Saviour's matchless love!

80. P. M.

1 What heavenly music falls sweet on my ear!
The strains how delightful! enchanted I hear
The voice of the angels, in chorus divine;
They sing of the Saviour; they sing he is mine!

2 Those harpers immortal invite me away;
They bid me to hasten—O, let me not stay:
I hear them all chanting, "Come, come to our shore.
Where trouble, and sorrow, and pain are no more."

3 O, fly, fly, ye moments, fly swiftly away;
Adieu, earthly pleasures, that fade in a day;
I hasten to mingle in that holy band,
Forever to dwell in the bright Eden land.

81.   L. M.

1 When for the eternal world I steer,
   And seas are calm and skies are clear,
   To faith in lively exercise,
   The distant hills all glorious rise.

CHORUS.—O then, with joy, I spread my sails,
   And fly before the wafting gales,
   To Canaan's shore,
   To Canaan's shore.
   And fly before the wafting gales
   To Canaan's shore.

2 With cheerful hope my eyes explore
   Each landmark on the distant shore;
   The tree of life, the pastures green,
   The golden street, the crystal stream.

3 When nearer still I draw to land,
   More eager all my powers expand;
   With steady helm and free-bent sail,
   The anchor drops within the veil!

82.   P. M.

1 O hail, happy day, that speaks our trials ended!
   Our Lord has come to take us home;
   O, hail, happy day!
   No more by doubts and fears distressed,
   We now shall gain our promised rest,
   And be forever blest. O, hail, happy day!

2 Swell loud the glad note, our bondage now is over:
   The Jubilee proclaims us free;
   O, hail, happy day!
   The day that brings a sweet release,
   That crowns our Jesus PRINCE OF PEACE,
   And bids our sorrows cease. O, hail, happy day!

3 O, hail, happy day, that ends our tears and sorrows,
   That brings us joy without alloy;
   O, hail, happy day!

There peace shall wave her sceptre high,
And love's fair banner greet the eye,
Proclaiming victory! O, hail, happy day!

4 Thrice hail, happy day, when earth shall smile in gladness,
And Eden bloom on nature's tomb;
O, hail, happy day!
Where life's pellucid waters glide,
We, by our dear Redeemer's side,
Forever shall abide. O, hail, happy day!

83. P. M.

1 How happy is the pilgrim's lot!
How free from every anxious thought,
From worldly hope and fear!
Confined to neither court or cell,
His soul disdains on earth to dwell;
He only sojourns here.

2 This happiness, in part, is mine,
Already saved from low design;
From every sinful love;
Blest with the scorn of carnal good,
My soul is lightened of its load,
And seeks the things above.

3 The things eternal I pursue;
A happiness beyond the view
Of those who basely pant;
For things by nature felt and seen—
Such honors, wealth and pleasures mean—
I neither have or want.

4 I have a house and portion fair!
My treasure and my heart are there—
There my abiding home,
And while on earth I make my stay,
I wait the swift approaching day
When Christ, my King, shall come.

84.   P. M.

1 Here on the earth as a stranger I roam;
   Here is no rest, is no rest;
Here as a pilgrim I wander alone,
   Yet I am blest, I am blest:
For I look forward to that glorious day,
When sin and sorrow will vanish away;
My heart doth leap while I hear Jesus say,
   There, there is rest, there is rest.

2 Here fierce temptations beset me around;
   Here is no rest, is no rest;
Here I am grieved while my foes me surround;
   Yet I am blest, I am blest:
Let them revile me and scoff at my name,
Laugh at my weeping, endeavor to shame;
I will go forward, for this is my theme,
   There, there is rest, there is rest.

3 This world of cares is a wilderness state;
   Here is no rest, is no rest;
Here I must bear from the world all its hate;
   Yet I am blest, I am blest.
Soon shall I be from the wicked released;
Soon shall the weary forever be blest;
Soon shall I lean upon Jesus' own breast;
   Then there is rest, there is rest.

85.   P. M.

1 There is a world to come,
   Happy and pure;
That is the Christian's home,
   Long to endure.
O, in that world of light
All shall be forever bright!
Faith views it with delight,
   Counting it sure.

2 There Christ will ever reign,
    All glorious King!
There music's rapturous strain
    Ever will ring;
Saints who in ages by
Suffered, and were called to die,
There in sweet harmony
    Anthems will sing.

3 There is our paradise,
    Eden restored;
All beauteous in their eyes
    Who love the Lord.
Wastes that are now most drear,
Like the rose shall blossom there,
And be a garden fair:
    Thus saith the word.

4 O, that bright world to come
    Tongue cannot tell!
Thrice blessed is the home
    Where saints will dwell;
Turn then from sin away,
And the word of God obey;
Then at the last great day
    All will be well.

86.

1 Jesus died, yet lives forever,
    O, hail his name!
Glory to the mighty Saviour,
    Who pleads for men!

2 Once he hung a bleeding offering,
    All bathed in wo,
To the world salvation proffering,
    Long time ago.

3 Now he sits in yonder heaven
    Proclaiming love.
All may have their sins forgiven
    By him above.

4 Soon this blest, propitious hour,
   Will pass away,
 And he come with awful power.
   O, fearful day!

5 Come, ye sinners, seek his favor
   Who died for you;
 O, embrace this blessed Saviour;
   His love is true.

87.   P. M.

1 Joyfully, joyfully, onward I move.
 Bound for the land of bright glory and love;
 Angelic choristers sing as I come,
 "Joyfully, joyfully, haste to thy home!"

2 Soon, with my pilgrimage ended below,
 On to the land of the blessed I go;
 Pilgrim and stranger no more shall I roam,
 Joyfully, joyfully, resting at home.

3 Friends fondly cherished, who greet me no more,
 Soon shall I meet on the fair blissful shore,
 Chanting in triumph past death's chilling gloom,
 Joyfully, joyfully resting at home.

4 Sounds of sweet music will fall on my ear;
 Heavenly harpings I ever shall hear,
 Ringing in harmony through the high dome,
 Joyfully, joyfully, in my blest home.

5 Death, with thy weapons of war, lay me low;
 Strike, king of terrrors, I fear not the blow!
 Jesus hath broken the bars of the tomb;
 Joyfully, joyfully, I shall go home.

6 Bright will the morn of eternity dawn;
 Death shall be banished, his sceptre be gone;
 Joyfully then shall I witness his doom,
 Joyfully, joyfully, safely at home!

88. C. M.

1 What vessel are you sailing in?
    Declare to us the same.
  Our vessel is the Ark of God,
    And Christ our Captain's name.

CHORUS.

  Hoist every sail to catch the gale—
    If calm, then ply the oar;
  The night begins to wear away.
    We soon shall reach the shore.

2 Say, are you not afraid some storm
    Your bark will overwhelm?
  We need not fear, the Lord is near;
    Our Captain holds the helm!

89. P. M.

1 Ye who rose to meet the Lord,
  Ventured on his faithful word,
  Faint not now, for your reward
    Will be quickly given.
  Faint not! always watch and pray;
  Jesus will not long delay;
  Even now the dawn of day
    Beams from yonder heaven.

2 Would ye to the end endure?
  Keep the wedding garment pure;
  Claim ye still the promise sure,
    Faithful is the Lord!
  Let your lamps be burning bright;
  In God's word is beaming light;
  Live by faith, and not by sight;
    Crowns are your reward.

3 Mid the darts of angry foe
  Onward, fearless, onward go;
  The good soldier's courage show;
    On to victory!

"Let thine eyes be turned to me,"
Jesus says. "I am with thee;
Overcome and faithful be;
   Thou shalt glory see."

4 Marriage supper all prepared,
By the guests will soon be shared,
In fair righteous robes arrayed
   Like the Bridegroom King.
Glory to Jehovah's name!
Sound aloud the glad acclaim;
To the Lamb that once was slain,
   Hallelujahs bring!

90.

1 Come, all ye friends of Zion,
   Who are waiting for salvation,
Have your lamps brightly burning,
   And attend the proclamation,
Saying, "All things now are ready
For the feeble and the needy;
All my fatlings now are killed,
And prepared on the table."

2 O, what a happy meeting,
   When salvation is completed,
And all tribulation ended,
   And the spotless robe prepared
For the Bride to be adorned,
By the jasper walls, when crowned,
Singing, "Worthy is the Lamb,"
In the New Jerusalem!

3 O sinner, be not doubting,
   While the holy ones are shouting;
Come and join the happy army,
   There is nothing that will harm you
If you follow Christ the Saviour,
And break off all bad behaviour,
And repent and be converted—
You may sing his praises too!

91. P. M.

1 Must Jesus bear the cross alone,
  And all his saints go free?
 There is a cross for every one;
  There is a cross for me.
 I love the cross of Calvary—
 Through which, by faith, the crown I see—
 To me sweet pardon bringing;
  That is the cross for me!

2 How faithful does the Saviour prove
  To those that serve him here!
 They now may taste his perfect love,
  And joy to hail him near.
 Yes, perfect love will dry our tears,
 And cast out all tormenting fears
 Which round our hearts are clinging;
  That is the love for me!

3 We hail the consecrated cross,
  For by it we are free;
 And by it we shall wear the crown,
  When we the Saviour see.
 There is a crown prepared above,
 The purchase of Redeeming love,
 For me at his appearing;
  That is the crown for me.

92. P. M.

1 How firm a foundation, ye saints of the Lord,
 Is laid for your faith in his excellent word!
 What more can he say than to you he hath said,
 You who unto Jesus for refuge have fled?

2 In every condition—in sickness, in health,
 In poverty's vale, or abounding in wealth,
 At home, or abroad, on the land, on the sea,—
 As thy days may demand, shall thy strength ever be.

3 When through fiery trials thy pathway shall lie,
 My grace all-sufficient shall be thy supply;

The flames shall not hurt thee; I only design
Thy dross to consume, and thy gold to refine.

4 The soul that on Jesus hath leaned for repose,
I will not, I will not, desert to his foes:
That soul, though all hell should endeavour to shake,
I will not, I will not, I will not forsake!

93. P. M.

Sweet bonds now unite all the children of peace
To their precious Jesus, whose love cannot cease;
And though, in his absence, in sadness we roam,
We hope to behold him in glory at home.

CHORUS.

Home, home, sweet, sweet home!
Prepare us, dear Saviour, for glory, our home.

94. P. M.

Come, thou fount of every blessing,
  Teach me to adore thy grace;
Streams of mercy never ceasing
  Call for songs of loudest praise.
O, to grace how great a debtor
  I am ever made to be!
Let that grace, Lord, like a fetter,
  Bind my wandering heart to thee.

95. P. M.

1 All the prophets of old did with rapture behold
  A bright vision of glory to come;
And apostles have told of the beauty and gold
  In the city prepared for our home.

CHORUS.

Hail, Saviour! dear Saviour! O Saviour, come!
Here we mourn, and we sigh, and we still ever cry.
Come and gather the faithful home.

2 O. we long to be there where no sorrow or care
   Shall disturb that sweet, heavenly rest!
  And we hope soon to share in those beauties so
   rare.
   In reserve for the good and the blest.

96. P. M.

1 Whither goest thou, pilgrim stranger,
   Wandering through this gloomy vale?
  Knowest thou it is full of danger?
   And will not thy courage fail?

CHORUS.
   I am bound for the kingdom.
   Will you go to glory with me?
   Hallelujah, praise ye the Lord.

2 Pilgrim thou dost justly call me,
   Passing through this desert wide,
  But no evil shall befall me
   While my Saviour is my guide.

97. P. M.

1 This groaning earth is too dark and drear
   For the saint's eternal home;
  But the city from heaven will soon be here:
  We know that the moment is drawing near
   When she in her glory shall come.
  Her gates of pearl we soon shall see,
   And her music we soon shall hear;
  Joyous and bright our home shall be
  We will rest in the shadow of life's fair tree,
   With our Saviour forever near.

2 We will gladly exchange a world like this,
   Where death triumphant reigns,
  For a home in that beautiful land of bliss
  Where all is happiness, joy and peace,
   And nothing can enter that pains.
  There is no more sorrow or gloomy night,

For the darkness shall pass away,
The glorious Lord shall be the light,
And the saints shall walk with him in white
In that happy and endless day.

3 O, there the loved of earth shall meet,
Whom death hath sundered here;
The prophets and patriarchs there will meet
With all that worship at Jesus' feet,
No more separation to fear.
Though trials and griefs await us here,
The conflict will soon be done:
This joyful hope our hearts shall cheer,
For we know that the Saviour will soon appear,
And leave us no longer alone.

98.   P. M.

1 How sweet to reflect on those joys that await me,
In yon blissful region, that haven of rest,
Where glorified spirits with welcome shall greet me.
And lead me to mansions prepared for the blest!
Encircled in light, and with glory enshrouded,
My happiness perfect, my mind's sky unclouded,
I there shall delight in the pleasures unbounded,
And range evermore through the Eden of love.

2 While angelic legions, with harps tuned celestial,
Harmoniously join in the concert of praise,
The saints as they flock, from the regions terrestrial,
In loud hallelujahs their voices will raise;
Then songs to the Lamb shall re-echo through heaven;
My soul will respond—to Immanuel be given
All honor, all glory, all might and dominion,
Who brought us by grace to the Eden of love.

3 O, hail, blessed state! hail, ye songsters of glory!
Ye harpers of bliss, I shall meet you above,
And join your full choir in rehearsing the story,
"Salvation from sorrow through Jesus' great love;"

Though prisoned in earth, yet by anticipation,
Already my soul feels a sweet prelibation
Of joys that await me, when freed from probation:
My spirit is now in the Eden of love!

99.   P. M.

1 The worst of sinners now may find,
A Saviour pitiful and kind,
  Who will them all receive!
None are too late who will repent;
Out of one sinner legions went;
  Jesus did him relieve.

2 Let all of us who know the Lord,
And taste the sweetness of his word,
  In Jesus' ways go on;
Our troubles and our conflicts here
Will only make us richer there,
  When we arrive at home.

100.   P. M.

1 Go, sinner, see the bleeding Lamb;—
  Will you go? will you go?
There is salvation in his name,—
  Will you go? will you go?
The crown of life you then shall wear,
And conqueror's palms you then shall bear!
And all the joys of glory share,—
  Will you go? will you go?

2 Ye weary, heavy-laden, come,—
  Will you go? will you go?
In mercy's house there yet is room,—
  Will you go? will you go?
The Lord is waiting to receive
All those who will on him believe,
He will thy conscience now relieve,—
  Will you go? will you go?

101. C. M.

1 What poor despised company
    Of travellers are these,
Who walk in yonder narrow way,
    Along the rugged maze?

2 Ah, these are of a royal line,
    All children of a King;
Heirs of immortal crowns divine,
    And lo, for joy they sing!

3 Why do they then appear so mean?
    And why so much despised?
Because of their rich robes unseen
    The world is not apprized.

4 But some of them seem poor, distressed.
    And lacking daily bread.
They are of boundless wealth possessed—
    With hidden manna fed,

5 But why keep they that narrow road,
    That rugged thorny maze?
That is the way their Leader trod;
    They love and keep his ways.

6 Why must they shun the pleasant path
    That worldlings love so well?
Because that is the way to death,
    The open road to hell.

102. P. M.

1 Hark! hark! hear the blest tidings;
    Soon, soon Jesus will come
Robed, robed in honor and glory,
    To gather his ransomed ones home:
    Yes, yes, O yes, to gather his ransomed ones home.

2 Joy, joy, sound it more loudly;
    Sing, sing glory to God;

Soon, soon Jesus is coming;
Publish the tidings abroad:
Yes, yes, O yes, publish the tidings abroad.

3 Bright, bright seraphs attending;
Shouts, shouts filling the air;
Down, down swiftly from heaven,
Jesus our Lord will appear.
Yes, yes, O yes, Jesus our Lord will appear.

4 Now, now, through a glass darkly,
Shine, shine visions to come;
Soon, soon we shall behold them,
Cloudless and bright in our home:
Yes, yes, cloudless and bright in our home.

103. P. M.

1 The chariot! the chariot! its wheels roll in fire,
As the Lord cometh down in the pomp of his ire;
Lo, self-moving it drives on the pathway of cloud,
And the heavens with the burden of Godhead are bowed.

2 The trumpet! the trumpet! the dead have all heard;
Lo, the dephs of the stone-covered charnel are stirred!
From the sea, from the earth, from East, West, South, and North,
All the vast generation of man are come forth.

3 The Judgment! the Judgment! the thrones are all set
Where the Lamb and the white-vested elders are met;
There all flesh is at once in the sight of the Lord,
And the doom of eternity hangs on his word.

4 O, mercy! O, mercy! look down from above,
Great Creator, on us, thy poor children, with love!
When beneath to their darkness the wicked are driven,
May our justified souls be in favor with heaven!

104.   L. M.

1 Awake, my soul, in joyful lays,
  And sing the great Redeemer's praise;
  He justly claims a song from me;
  His loving-kindness, O, how free!

2 He saw me ruined by the fall,
  Yet loved me notwithstanding all;
  He saved me from my lost estate;
  His loving-kindness, O, how great!

3 Though numerous hosts of mighty foes—
  Though earth and hell my ways oppose,
  He safely leads my foes along;
  His loving-kindness, O, how strong!

4 When trouble, like a gloomy cloud,
  Has gathered thick and thundered loud,
  He has forever by me stood;
  His loving-kindness, O, how good!

5 When from his love I go astray
  He leaves me not in folly's way,
  His tenderness doth then appear;
  His loving-kindness, O, how dear!

6 When from the skies he shall descend,
  And round him angel hosts attend,
  Then may I through his boundless grace,
  His loving-kindness ever praise!

105.   P. M.

1 I am sighing for home where the King in his glory
  Shall banish all sorrow and scatter all gloom:
  I sigh for the land where the youth and the hoary
  Shall dwell in bright Eden, forever at home.

CHORUS.

Sweet home, sweet home, sweet home, sweet home,
O, there let me dwell, in that bright Eden home.

2 I am sighing for home where the songs of the ransomed
  Shall echo their strains throughout heaven's high dome!
 I sigh for the day when all hearts shall be gladdened,
 And the pilgrims be resting in their happy home.

3 I am sighing for home, where no ties shall be broken,
  Where death shall not enter, or sickness be known.
 I sigh for the day of which prophets have spoken:
 The blest restitution—I long to go home!

106. P. M.

1 Hail, the good time coming, lo, it draweth nigh,
  When the pilgrims shall be blest;
 When Christ shall reign through all the earth,
  And bring the promised rest.

CHORUS.
Then hasten, Lord, hasten the glorious day,
When the saints shall possess all the earth restored
And reign with their Lord evermore.

2 Hail, the good time coming, when the curse shall cease,
  And the tree of life shall grow;
 When the earth shall smile in Eden bloom,
  And the crystal streams shall flow.

3 Hail, the good time coming, when the meek shall rejoice
  That the earth's dread night is no more;
 When oppression, and sorrow, and sickness, and death,
  Shall never again reach our shore.

107. P. M.

1 Hear the last call of mercy, that lingers for thee;
 O! sinner, receive it, to Jesus now flee!
 He often has called thee, but thou hast refused!
 His offered salvation and love is abused!

2 Hear the last call of mercy, O, turn not away,
For now swiftly hasteth the dread vengeance day!
The Spirit invites you, and pleading, says, Come!
O, come to life's waters, nor thirstingly roam.

3 Hear the last call of mercy, O, steel not thy heart.
For mercy is rising from earth to depart!
Thy Saviour is calling, "Ye weary ones come,
O, come and be ransomed, in me there is room."

4 Hear the last call of mercy, that lingers for thee;
Now leave thy sad bondage, O, sinner be free!
Say not in thy mourning, "The harvest is past,
The summer is ended," and perish at last.

108.   P. M.

1 O, happy hour! I know the Lord is mine!
    All is well. All is well.
He saves me now by his great power divine.
    All is well. All is well.
From henceforth all for Christ I give,
Resolved for him alone to live:
His precious word I do believe.
    All is well. All is well.

2 O, what is earth, this earth, when I can sing
    All is well. All is well.
Vain are the joys, the joys that sense can bring.
    All is well. All is well.
Great are my transport, light, and rest,
When I am by my Saviour blest,
And he invites me to his breast.
    All is well. All is well.

3 When duty calls, I will, I will obey.
    All is well. All is well.
Welcome the cross! the cross along my way.
    All is well. All is well.
Though fearful nature shrinking stand,
Lord, I am thine, and in thy hand,
And I will move at thy command.
    All is well. All is well.

4 Rise, rise, my soul, press onward, onward still.
    All is well. All is well.
God shall my powers with all his fulness fill.
    All is well. All is well.
Stronger than death, his love to me
Shall be my joy eternally,
And I shall all his glory see.
    All is well. All is well.

109.   S. M.

1 How sweet is Jesus' name!
  How sweet is Jesus' name!
  Let saints delight, with angels bright,
  His mercy to proclaim.

CHORUS.

All hail, salvation free! All hail, salvation free!
Salvation free to you and me;
All hail salvation free.

2 Upon the cross he died,
  Upon the cross he died,
  Yet lives again, O, praise his name!
  He lives—the crucified!

3 He offers life to all,
  He offers life to all,
  O, let us bow before him now,
  And for this favor call.

4 Who will refuse his love?
  Who will refuse his love?
  O, sinner, hear the Saviour dear,
  He calls you from above.

110.   P. M.

1 The pleasures of earth I have seen fade away;
They bloom for a season, but soon they decay;
But pleasures more lasting by Jesus are given,
Salvation on earth, and a mansion in heaven.

2 Allure me no longer, ye false glowing charms;
  The Saviour invites me—I go to his arms;
  At the banquet of mercy I hear there is room;
  O, there may I feast with his children at home!

3 I sigh from this body of sin to be free,
  Which hinders, dear Lord, my communion with thee;
  Though now my temptations like billows may foam,
  All, all will be past when I am with thee at home.

4 While here in this valley of conflict I stay,
  O, grant me submission and strength as my day:
  In all my afflictions to thee I will come,
  Rejoicing in hope of my glorious home.

111.   P. M.

1 How long, O Lord, our Saviour,
    Wilt thou remain away?
  Our hearts are growing weary
    Of thy so long delay:
  O when shall come the moment
    When brighter far than morn,
  The sunshine of thy glory
    The heavens shall adorn?

2 How long, O gracious Master,
    Wilt thou thy household leave?
  So long hast thou now tarried,
    Few thy return believe.
  Immersed in sloth and folly,
    How many, Lord, we see!
  And few of us stand ready
    With joy to welcome thee.

3 O, wake thy slumbering virgins,
    Send forth the solemn cry—
  Let all the saints repeat it—
    "The Bridegroom draweth nigh."
  May all our lamps be burning,
    Our loins well girded be,
  That we at thy returning,
    With joy thy face may see.

112. P. M.

1 A fountain in Jesus, which runs always free
Is opened for cleansing such sinners as we!
Our sins, though like crimson, as white as the wool
Are made at this fountain, which always is full.

2 All things now are ready, he invites us to come!
A feast is here made by the Father and Son;
Rich dainties abundant here we may receive,
And pleasures forever, if we will believe.

3 The guests who were bidden refused the call;
For they were not willing or ready at all
To be stripped of their honor, and part with their store,
For a supper prepared for the vile and the poor.

4 If they are not ready, and wish to delay,
" My house shall be filled," the Father doth say,
" From the highways and hedges, the halt and the blind
Shall come, and be welcome, as they are inclined."

113. L. M.

1 Hail, wondrous love, that first began
The scheme to rescue fallen man.
Hail, matchless, free, eternal grace,
That made for me a hiding-place!

2 Against that God who rules on high,
The purpose of my heart did lie;
I fought the counsels of his grace—
Too proud to seek a hiding-place!

3 Encompassed with a fearful night,
And fond of darkness more than light,
Madly I ran a sinful race,
Despising mercy's hiding-place!

4 But lo, a heavenly voice I heard,
And Jesus to my soul appeared,
And offered me his saving grace,
And thus became my hiding-place!

5 And now my God is all my joy;
His work is my divine employ;
His word with rapture I embrace,
And sing of a sweet hiding-place!

114. P. M.

1 Son of God, thy people's shield,
  Must we still thine absence mourn?
Let thy promise be fulfilled;
  Thou hast said, "I will return."

2 Gracious Master, soon appear,
  Quickly bring the morning light;
Then will cease the constant tear,
  Hope be turned to joyful sight.

3 As a woman counts the days
  Till her absent lord she see,
Longs and watches, weeps and prays,
  So the church must long for thee.

4 Come, that we may see thee nigh,
  Then thy flock shall feed in peace;
Hushed forever trouble's sigh,
  Sin and sorrow's triumph cease.

115. P. M.

1 Jesus, I my cross have taken,
  All to leave and follow thee;
Naked, poor, despised, forsaken,
  Thou, henceforth, my all shalt be!
Perish every fond ambition—
  All that I have sought or known;
Yet how rich is my condition!
  God and heaven are now my own.

2 Let the world despise and leave me—
  They have left my Saviour too;
Human hearts deceive me sorely,—
  Thou art not, like them, untrue;
And whilst thou shalt smile upon me,
  God of wisdom, love and might,
Foes may hate and friends disown me;
  Show thy face and all is bright.

3 Go, then, earthly fame and treasure;
  Come, disaster, scorn and pain:
In thy service pain is pleasure;
  With thy favor loss is gain.
I have called thee Abba, Father,
  I have set my heart on thee;
Let the storm-clouds round me gather,
  Thou shalt my protection be.

4 Soul, then know thy full salvation;
  Triumph over sin and fear;
Joy to find in every station
  Something still to do or bear.
Think what Spirit helps thee freely:
  Think what Father's smiles are thine—
Think that Jesus died to win thee.
  Child of heaven, canst thou repine?

116. P. M.

1 Begone, unbelief, my Saviour is near!
And for my relief will surely appear:
By prayer let me wrestle, and he will perform:
With Christ in my vessel, I smile at the storm.

2 Though dark be my way, since he is my guide,
Mine is to obey, his is to provide:
Though cisterns be broken, and creatures all fail,
The word he has spoken will surely prevail.

3 Why should I complain of want or distress,
Temptation or pain? he told me no less!
The heirs of salvation, I know from his word,
Through much tribulation must follow the Lord.

4 How bitter the cup, no heart can conceive,
  Which he drank quite up, that sinners might live!
  His way was much darker and rougher than mine;
  Did Jesus thus suffer, and shall I repine?

5 Since all that I meet shall work for my good,
  The bitter is sweet, the medicine is food;
  Though painful at present it will not last long,
  And then, O, how pleasant the conqueror's song!

117.   L. M.

1 When I survey the wondrous cross,
    On which the Prince of glory died,
  My richest gain I count but loss,
    And pour contempt on all my pride.

2 Forbid it, Lord, that I should boast,
    Save in thy death, thou Just and Good!
  All the vain things which charm me most,
    I leave them for thy precious blood.

3 See from his head, his hands, his feet,
    Sorrow and love flow mingled down!
  When did such love and sorrow meet,
    Or thorns compose so rich a crown?

4 Were the whole realm of nature mine,
    That were an offering far too small;
  Love so amazing, so divine,
    Demands my heart, my life, my all!

118.   L. M.

1 When strangers stand and hear me tell
    What glories in my Saviour dwell,
  Where he has gone they fain would know,
    That they may seek and love him too.

2 O, may my spirit daily rise,
    On faith, to him above the skies,
  Till I shall make my last remove,
    To dwell forever with my Love.

3 His gospel bears my spirit up,
    While I expect that blessed hope—
  The bright appearance of the Lord,
    And faith stands leaning on his word.

4 Come, my Beloved, haste away,
    Cut short the hours of thy delay;
  Fly, like a youthful hart or roe,
    Over the hills where beauties grow!

119.   P. M.

1 Hear the glorious proclamation,
  The glad tidings of salvation,
  Hear the glorious proclamation
    Of the Saviour near.

CHORUS.

  While the choir of angels,
  While the choir of angels,
  While the choir of angels,
    Shall be sounding through the air.

2 Hark! the tidings onward rolling,
  Jesus comes, the world controlling!
  Hark! the tidings onward rolling,
    Jesus comes to reign.

3 See the "sign" in heaven appearing,
  And the blazing chariot nearing,
  See the "sign" in heaven appearing,
    And the Saviour there.

4 See the earth in terror shaking,
  And the dead to life awaking,
  See the earth in terror shaking,
    And the dead arise.

5 Now on wings of light ascending,
  With a shining host attending,
  Now on wings of light ascending,
    Mount up to the skies.

6 See the banner waves in glory,
  While ten thousand tell the story,
  See the banner waves in glory,
    And the saints all there.

120. P. M.

1 We speak of the realms of the blest;
    Of that country so bright and so fair;
  And oft are its glories confest;
    But what must it be to be there?

2 We speak of its pathway of gold;
    Of its wall decked with jewels so rare;
  Of its wonders and pleasures untold;
    But what must it be to be there?

3 We speak of its freedom from sin,
    From sorrow, temptation and care,
  From trials without and within;
    But what must it be to be there?

4 We speak of its service of love;
    Of the robes which the glorified wear;
  Of the raptures which every heart move;
    But what must it be to be there?

5 May we, then, midst pleasure or wo,
    For that kingdom our hearts now prepare;
  And shortly we also shall know,
    And feel what it is to be there.

121. P. M.

1 On the high cliffs of Jordan with pleasure I stand,
  And view in prospective the fair promised land;
  The land where the ransomed with singing shall come,
  And enter the Kingdom prepared as their home.

2 All over those peaceful, delectable plains,
  The Lord our Redeemer in righteousness reigns;
  His sceptre of empire he now doth assume,
  And kindly doth welcome his followers home.

3 How blest are those regions, the realms of repose,
   Where with fruits, O, how grateful, the "tree of
      life" grows;
   The regions ambrosial forever in bloom,
   God's own habitation, the saints' happy home!

4 Those pleasures of glory, O, when shall I share,
   And crowns of celestial felicity wear;
   And range those bright landscapes, exempt from a
      sigh,
   The home of our fathers, now specially nigh!

122.   P. M.

1 O the amazing change!
     A world created new!
   My thoughts with transport range
     The lovely scene to view:
   Thee, Lord divine, in all I trace;
   The work is thine—thine be the praise.

2 When pointed brambles grew,
     Entwined with horrid thorn,
   Gay flowers, forever new,
     The painted fields adorn;
   The lily there, and blushing rose,
   In union fair their sweets disclose.

3 Where the bleak mountain stood,
     All bare and disarrayed,
   See the wide branching wood
     Diffuse its grateful shade;
   Tall oaks, and pines, and cedars nod,
   And elms and vines confess their God.

4 The tyrants of the plain
     Shall cease their savage roar;
   No more they rend the slain,
     They thirst for blood no more;
   But infant hands fierce tigers lead,
   And lions with the oxen feed.

5 O, when, almighty Lord,
　　Shall these glad scenes arise,
　To verify thy word,
　　And bless our wondering eyes;
　That earth, with all her tongues, may raise
　United songs of ardent praise?

123.   P. M.

1 Hail, thou blest morn,
　　When Christ the Mediator,
　Welcomed by angels,
　Cradled in a manger,
　Came, a Redeemer
　For the ruined nations,
　　Bringing their ransom!

2 See, the bright star,
　　High over Judah's mountains,
　Pours down its splendor
　On the joyful vision
　Of the enraptured,
　Watchful men of wisdom,
　　Beaming salvation.

3 Come, pay your homage
　　To the Infant Mighty!
　Hark! hosts celestial
　Sing above most sweetly,
　"Glory and peace," which
　Shall be everlasting:
　　Amen, and amen!

4 Say, shall we bring
　　To him, in our devotion,
　Gems of the mountains,
　Odors of the islands,
　Pearls, gold, or silver?
　He demands the offering
　　Of our affections.

124.   L. M.

1 God of my life, to thee I call;
Afflicted, at thy feet I fall;
When floods of sorrow thus prevail,
Leave not my trembling heart to fail.

2 Friend of the friendless and the faint,
Where should I lodge my deep complaint?
Where, but with thee, whose open door
Invites the helpless and the poor.

3 Did ever mourner plead with thee
And thou refuse that mourner's plea?
Does not the word, still fixed, remain,
That none shall seek thy face in vain?

4 Poor though I am, despised, forgot,
Yet God, my God, forgets me not;
That soul is safe, and must succeed,
For whom the Lord vouchsafes to plead.

125.   S. M.

1 How tender is thy hand,
  O thou most gracious Lord!
Afflictions come at thy command,
  And leave us at thy word.

2 How gentle was the rod
  That chastened us for sin!
How soon we found a smiling God
  Where deep distress had been.

3 A Father's hand we felt,
  A Father's love we knew,
When full of penitence we knelt,
  And found his promise true.

4 Now will we bless the Lord,
  And in his strength confide;
Forever be his name adored,
  For there is none beside.

126.　　　　P. M.

1 O, come, come away! for time's career is closing;
Let worldly care henceforth forbear;
　　O, come, come away!
Come, come, our holy joys renew,
Where love and heavenly friendship grew;
The Spirit welcomes you;
　　O, come, come away!

2 Awake ye, awake! no time now for reposing;
"The Lord is near!" breaks on the ear;
　　O, come, come away!
Come, come where Jesus' love will be,
Who says, "I meet with two or three;"
Sweet promise made to thee.
　　O, come, come away!

3 Come where sacred song the pilgrim's heart is cheering;
Come, and learn there the power of prayer;
　　O, come, come away!
In sweetest notes of sympathy
We praise and pray in harmony;
Love makes our unity.
　　O, come, come away!

4 Night soon will be past, and endless day appearing,
Away from home no more we roam;
　　O, come, come away!
And when the trump of God shall sound,
The saints no more by death are bound;
We own our Jesus crowned.
　　O, come, come away!

5 O, come, come away, my Saviour, in thy glory!
"Thy kingdom come, thy will be done;"
　　O, come, come away!
O, come, my Lord, thy right maintain,
And take thy throne and on it reign!
Then earth shall bloom again.
　　O, come, come away!

INDEX.

	HYMN.
All hail the great Immanuel's	2
Awake, and sing the song	3
Am I a soldier	33
Away with our sorrow	54
Are we almost there	75
All the prophets of old	95
Amazing grace	39
Awake, my soul, in joyful	104
A fountain in Jesus	112
Broad is the road	8
Before Jehovah's awful	15
Beside the gospel pool	27
Begone, unbelief	116
Come, ye sinners	18
Come, let us anew	35
Come, all ye friends of Zion	90
Come, thou fount	94
Drooping souls	66
Equip me for the war	32
Father of mercies, in thy	22
From whence doth this union	48
God, in the gospel of	14
Go, sinners, see the bleeding	100
God of my life	124

Hail, wondrous love	113
Hark! the song	10
Hark! whence that voice	13
High in the heavens	40
How perfect is thy word	42
How happy are the little	63
Hail to the brightness	78
How happy is the pilgrim's	83
Here on the earth as a	84
How firm a foundation	92
How sweet to reflect	98
Hark! hark! hear the blest	102
Hail, the good time coming	106
Hear the last call of mercy	107
How sweet is Jesus' name	109
How long, O Lord, our Saviour	111
Hear the glorious	119
Hail, thou blest	123
How tender is	125
In expectation sweet	7
In Eden's bowers	20
In the sun	45
In evil long	37
I am sighing for home	105
Jesus, refuge of my	5
Jesus, at thy command	36
Jehovah reigns	43
Jesus died, yet	86
Joyfully, joyfully	87
Jesus, I my cross	115
Kingdoms and thrones	41
Lord, in thy temple	16
Lo, he comes	44
My soul is happy when	46
My heavenly home is	67
My days are gliding	70
Mark that pilgrim	74
Must Jesus bear	91

INDEX.

O thou, from whom	4
O thou, to whose all-searching	6
O thou, in whose presence	12
O, how happy are they	21
O, for a faith that	38
On Jordan's	49
On the mountain's	62
Out on an ocean	73
O God, my inmost	76
O, hail happy day	82
O, how I long	61
O, happy hour, I know	108
On the high cliffs	121
O the amazing change	122
O, come, come	126
Praise God, from whom	1
Show pity, Lord	19
Stand up, my soul	30
Soldiers of the	34
Salem's great King	60
Sweet bonds	93
Son of God, thy people's	114
There is a King of	9
To-day the Saviour	17
Thine oath and	24
There is a fountain	26
The Christian warrior	28
The glorious day is coming	47
There is a land of calm	50
The last lovely	55
The voice of free	57
The Lord our God is clothed	59
Together let us sweetly	68
The gospel trumpet	71
Thou Judge of	77
There is a world to	85
This groaning	97
The worst of sinners	99
The chariot	103
The pleasures of earth I have	110

Watchman! tell us	11
What shall I render	23
When marshalled on	25
Wait on the Lord	29
When I can read my	31
Will you go, sinner, go	51
What heavenly music do	52
When shall the voice	53
When the last trumpet's	56
With joy we meditate	58
When shall I see the day	65
We are bound for the land	72
We are going home, led by	79
What heavenly music falls	80
When for the eternal	81
What vessel	88
Whither goest thou	96
We have heard from	64
What poor, despised	101
When I survey the wondrous	117
When strangers stand	118
We speak of the realms	120
Ye valiant soldiers	69
Ye, who rose to meet	89